This Book
Belongs to

_____

_____

_____

A Celestial Coincidence: Solar eclipses happen when the Moon moves between the Earth and the Sun, covering the Sun and casting a shadow on the Earth. It's like the Moon playing hide and seek with the Sun!

Types of Solar Eclipses: There are three main types: total, partial, and annular. In a total eclipse, the Sun is completely hidden by the Moon. During a partial eclipse, only part of the Sun is covered. An annular eclipse occurs when the Sun looks like a ring of fire in the sky!

The Path of Totality: Only people in the "path of totality" can see a total solar eclipse. This path is where the Moon's shadow completely covers the Sun. It's a narrow strip that changes with every eclipse.

Baily's Beads Effect: Just before and after a total solar eclipse, you can see tiny spots of light on the edge of the Moon's shadow. These are called Baily's Beads, caused by the sunlight peeking through the Moon's rugged terrain.

The Diamond Ring Effect: Right before a total eclipse becomes complete, or just as it ends, the Sun's light can shine through a valley on the Moon's surface, creating a bright spot that looks like a diamond ring in the sky.

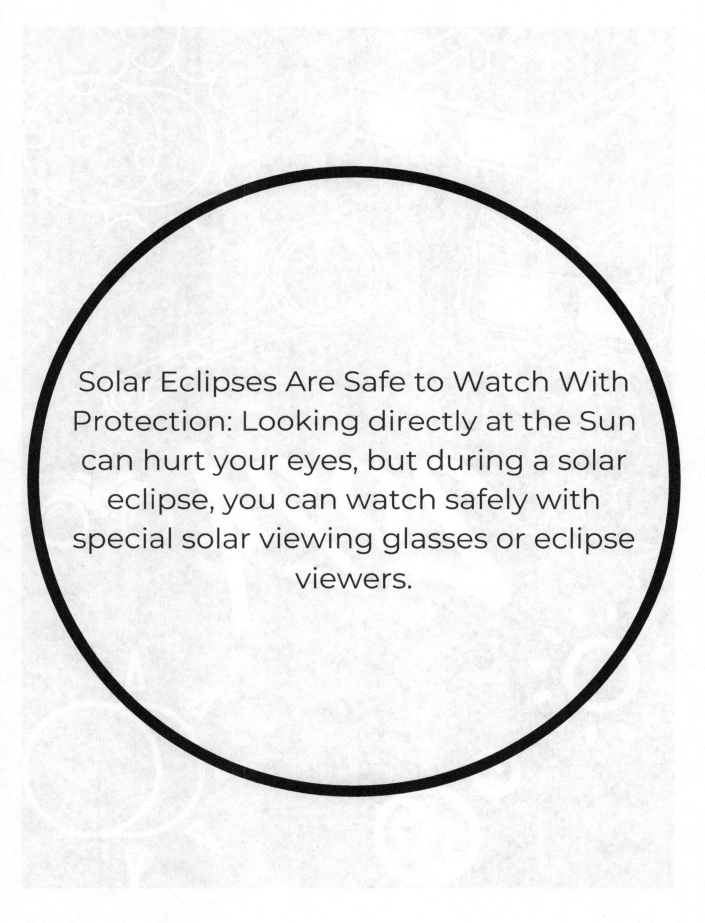

Solar Eclipses Are Safe to Watch With Protection: Looking directly at the Sun can hurt your eyes, but during a solar eclipse, you can watch safely with special solar viewing glasses or eclipse viewers.

Eclipses Don't Happen Every Month: Even though the Moon orbits the Earth about once a month, we don't have a solar eclipse every month because the Moon's orbit is tilted. So, it's not always perfectly aligned between the Earth and the Sun

Ancient Times and Eclipses: Long ago, people were scared of solar eclipses because they didn't understand them. Many cultures thought eclipses were a sign that something bad was going to happen.

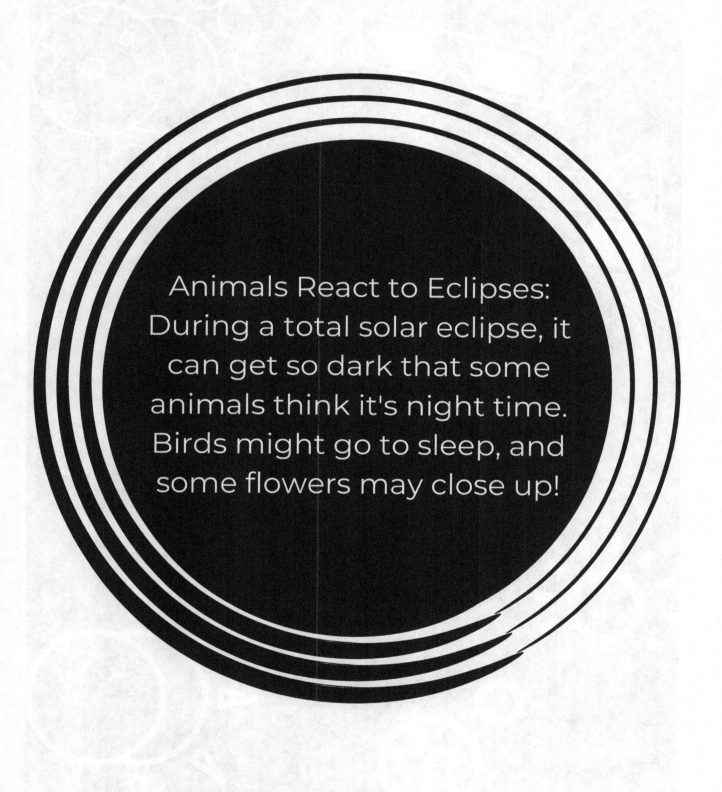

Animals React to Eclipses: During a total solar eclipse, it can get so dark that some animals think it's night time. Birds might go to sleep, and some flowers may close up!

Ancient Eclipse Predictions: The ancient Greeks were among the first to predict solar eclipses. One of the most famous predictors was Thales of Miletus, who predicted a solar eclipse in 585 BCE. This knowledge showed how advanced they were in understanding the heavens.

Speed of the Moon's Shadow: During a total solar eclipse, the Moon's shadow moves across the Earth's surface at speeds of up to 1,700 km/h (about 1,056 miles per hour)! Despite this speed, totality (when the Sun is completely covered) can last up to 7.5 minutes in one place.

Future Eclipses: If you miss one solar eclipse, don't worry! Scientists can predict when and where solar eclipses will happen years in advance. There's likely to be one visible from some part of the Earth every 18 months or so.

Solar Eclipses on Other Planets: Solar eclipses don't just happen on Earth. Any planet with moons can experience them, but since Earth's Moon is just the right size and distance, solar eclipses here are uniquely spectacular.

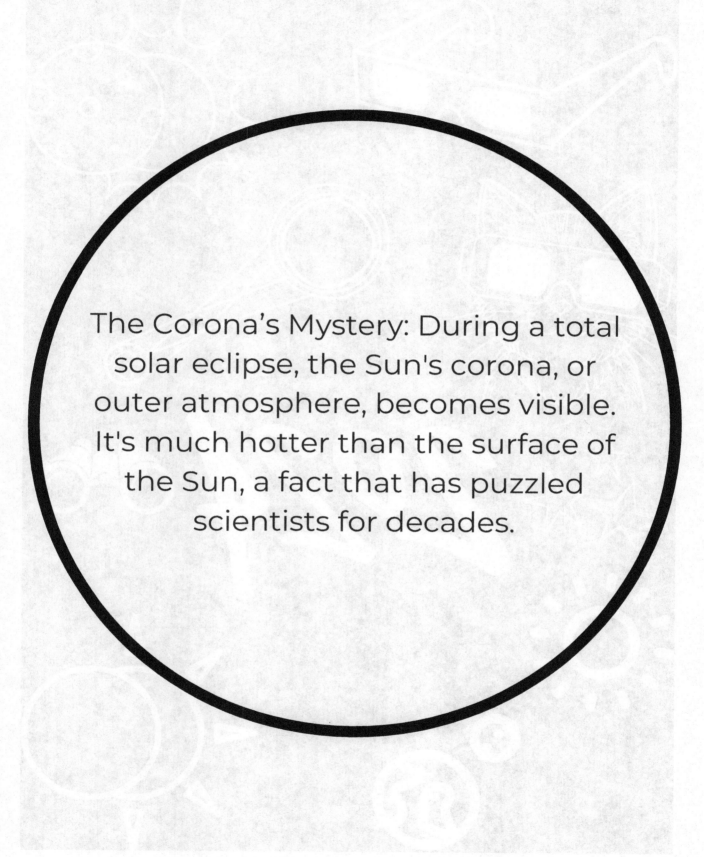

The Corona's Mystery: During a total solar eclipse, the Sun's corona, or outer atmosphere, becomes visible. It's much hotter than the surface of the Sun, a fact that has puzzled scientists for decades.

Eclipse Chasing: Some people love solar eclipses so much that they travel around the world to see them. These "eclipse chasers" go to great lengths to experience the brief moments of totality.

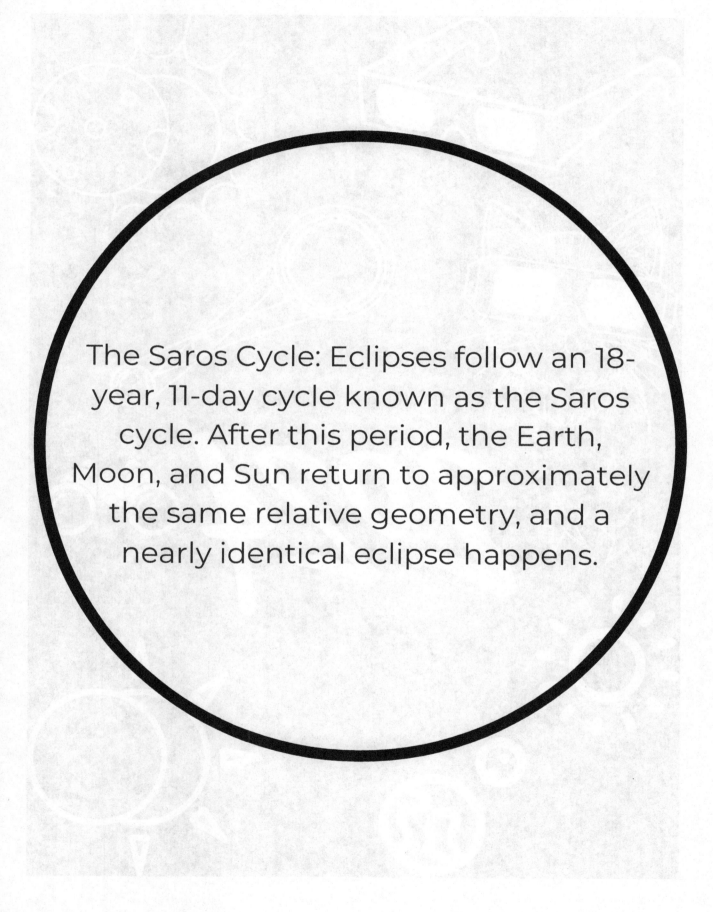

The Saros Cycle: Eclipses follow an 18-year, 11-day cycle known as the Saros cycle. After this period, the Earth, Moon, and Sun return to approximately the same relative geometry, and a nearly identical eclipse happens.

Impact on Solar Power: During a solar eclipse, areas that rely heavily on solar power may experience a drop in electricity production. Power grids have to prepare for this temporary loss by increasing output from other power sources.

First Photograph of a Solar Eclipse: The first photograph of a solar eclipse was taken on July 28, 1851, by Johann Julius Friedrich Berkowski. This was a major milestone in the field of astrophotography.

Eclipse-Induced Weather Changes: During a total solar eclipse, the drop in sunlight can cause a noticeable drop in temperature, often referred to as the "eclipse chill." It can also affect wind patterns temporarily.

Rare Hybrid Eclipses: Sometimes, an eclipse can be both total and annular along different sections of its path. This rare phenomenon is known as a hybrid eclipse and occurs because of variations in the distance between the Earth and the Moon.

Solar Eclipses in Literature and Myth: Throughout history, solar eclipses have been featured in myths, legends, and literature, often interpreted as omens or divine interventions. For example, in Homer's "Odyssey," an eclipse is seen as a sign from the gods

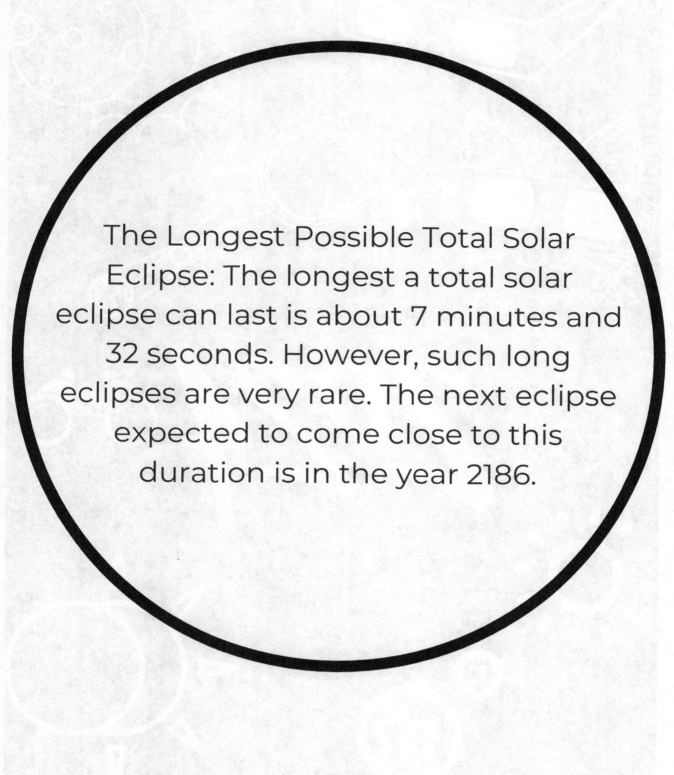

The Longest Possible Total Solar Eclipse: The longest a total solar eclipse can last is about 7 minutes and 32 seconds. However, such long eclipses are very rare. The next eclipse expected to come close to this duration is in the year 2186.

Eclipse Stamps: Some countries issue special postage stamps to commemorate significant solar eclipses. These stamps sometimes have unique features, like heat-sensitive ink that reveals the hidden image of the eclipse when warmed by touch.

International Space Station Observations: Astronauts aboard the International Space Station (ISS) have the unique opportunity to observe solar eclipses from space, offering a different perspective. They can see the Moon's shadow cast on the Earth's surface.

Solar Eclipses and Animal Behavior: Not only do some animals become quiet during totality, but others may become confused or show signs of agitation. The sudden darkness can disrupt their sense of time.

Chasing the Shadow: Some eclipse enthusiasts take to the skies in airplanes to chase the Moon's shadow during a solar eclipse, extending the duration of totality by flying along the path of the eclipse.

Eclipse Magnitude and Obscuration: The magnitude of a solar eclipse is the fraction of the Sun's diameter obscured by the Moon, while obscuration is the fraction of the Sun's area covered. These terms help astronomers describe the eclipse's appearance.

Ancient Eclipse Records: Chinese astronomers kept detailed records of solar eclipses over thousands of years. These historical documents are invaluable for current astronomical research, helping to refine our understanding of Earth's rotation over millennia.

Safety First: Never look directly at the Sun without proper eye protection, not just during an eclipse but at any time. Permanent eye damage can occur. Special eclipse glasses that filter out harmful solar radiation are essential for safe viewing.

Eclipses in Pop Culture: Solar eclipses have been depicted in movies, TV shows, and songs, often as pivotal plot points or as metaphors for change, mystery, or romance. They continue to captivate our imagination across various forms of media.

Eclipses and Solar Research:
Solar eclipses offer scientists
unique opportunities to study
the Sun's outer atmosphere, the
corona, which is usually
obscured by the bright light of
the Sun's surface. Observations
during eclipses have led to
discoveries about the Sun's
structure and behavior

Historical Eclipse Expeditions: Throughout history, scientists have embarked on expeditions to observe solar eclipses from the best vantage points. These journeys have contributed significantly to our understanding of astronomy, physics, and the universe.

Eclipse-Induced Tides: The gravitational pull of the Sun and Moon during an eclipse can slightly affect Earth's tides. While not dramatically different from normal tides, these "eclipse tides" are a fascinating example of the interconnectedness of celestial bodies.

Solar Eclipse Glasses: The only safe way to look directly at the uneclipsed or partially eclipsed Sun is through special-purpose solar filters, such as "eclipse glasses" or handheld solar viewers. Regular sunglasses, even very dark ones, are not safe for looking at the Sun.

The First Predicted Eclipse. The first solar eclipse predicted by scientists occurred in 585 BCE. It was predicted by Thales of Miletus, a Greek philosopher, which helped to halt a battle between the Medes and the Lydians, as they took the eclipse as a sign to cease fighting.

Photographing an Eclipse: Capturing a solar eclipse through photography requires special equipment, such as solar filters, to protect the camera's sensor from the intense sunlight. Many photographers also use long lenses to capture detailed images of the eclipse phases.

Eclipse Maps and Predictions: Modern astronomers can predict eclipses years in advance with great precision. They create maps showing the path of totality and the times the eclipse will occur, helping observers plan where and when to view the eclipse.

Influence on Temperature: During a total solar eclipse, the temperature can drop significantly in the path of totality, sometimes by as much as 15°F (8°C). This sudden change can feel like a rapid transition from day to night.

The Sun's Chromosphere: Just before totality in a solar eclipse, a thin ring of the Sun's chromosphere becomes visible. This layer glows a reddish color and is usually obscured by the brighter photosphere.

Solar Eclipses in the Ancient World: Ancient civilizations often interpreted solar eclipses as supernatural events or messages from the gods. These interpretations were recorded in various artifacts, such as stones, bones, and writings, providing insight into historical perspectives on eclipses.

Eclipse Megamovies: A recent initiative involves creating "eclipse megamovies" by stitching together images and videos of the solar eclipse taken by thousands of volunteers across the path of totality. This project aims to provide a detailed, high-resolution study of the Sun's corona and dynamics during an eclipse.

The Diamond Ring Through Time: The phenomenon of the diamond ring effect has been depicted in art and described in literature for centuries, serving as a source of inspiration and awe. This fleeting moment, occurring just before and after totality, symbolizes the transient beauty of celestial events.

Eclipse Shadows and Leaf Pinholes: During a partial solar eclipse, if you stand under a leafy tree, you can see hundreds of tiny crescent suns projected on the ground. These are images of the partially eclipsed Sun, created by light filtering through the small gaps between the leaves, acting as natural pinhole cameras.

Coronal Mass Ejections (CMEs) Visibility: Solar eclipses provide a unique opportunity for astronomers to observe coronal mass ejections (CMEs) — giant bubbles of gas and magnetic fields from the Sun — without the need for specialized instruments that artificially block the solar disk. This can lead to better understanding of solar storms and their impact on Earth.

Ancient Eclipse Predictors: The ancient Mayans were also skilled at predicting solar and lunar eclipses. They used sophisticated astronomical knowledge encoded in their calendars, notably the Dresden Codex, to forecast these events with remarkable accuracy.

Made in the USA
Las Vegas, NV
02 April 2024

88164093R00050